How to communicate your feelings with your partner (without fighting)

AGNES BAKER

Table of content

How to communicate your feelings with your partner (without fighting)

Have you ever been in a heated disagreement with your spouse and felt as though you were repeating the same points of contention without making any progress? Here are five tried-and-true methods for effectively communicating with your spouse, partner, husband, or wife and ending disputes.

What to Expect

This book offers five tried-and-true strategies for interacting peacefully:

#1: Determine what you need.

#2: Allow the storm to pass

#3: Be clear about what you require.

#4: Convey a strategy.

#5: Appreciate your partner's work.

You feel as though you are stuck at a crossroads. You're not moving forward, the situation is growing hotter, and you're beginning to say things you don't mean. Your spouse or partner doesn't understand your needs, and attempting to resolve the issue through conversation only makes matters worse.

We all engage in it! Any relationship will inevitably encounter conflict.

However, how do you stop an argument from starting and calm down long enough to speak with your husband?

It may be difficult to imagine a life in which you and your partner can speak without bickering, especially if this is the case now.

However, I can guarantee you that it is doable.

I've put together five easy, efficient, and tried-and-true techniques to help your spouse realize what you need and break the pattern of fighting to give you a head start. Understanding and putting into practice these vital communication skills can ease uncomfortable situations where attempting to talk things out just results in more arguments and can help you leave difficult conversations with your husband, wife, or partner feeling valued and understood.

It's crucial that you comprehend the distinction between arguing and communicating before you can overcome that barrier.

The distinction between arguing and communicating

In my practice, I interact with many married couples who are unaware of the small distinction between arguing and conversing. You're most angry when you're arguing in a confrontation. As the tension grows, everything suddenly gets worse. Our "fight or flight" system naturally drives us to either hold our ground and engage in combat or flee.

The rational part of our brain briefly shuts down when we feel threatened, even merely verbally or emotionally, in order to defend ourselves against the attack and work out how to go back to a position where we are emotionally safe. This system not only responds to physical threats but also to emotional rage, so any perceived assault from your partner will set off this reaction.

But the issue with this attitude is that it makes it difficult for us to express our needs clearly.

Although it may seem like a natural way to defend yourself, saying "This isn't my fault" or "I don't know what you're talking about" actually leads to a vicious loop of argumentation.

Two factors are frequently at play when it comes to finding that tranquil place:

1. We don't always understand what we require to deescalate a conflict; and

2. Even if we do know what we need, it might be difficult to express it to your spouse in a way that they can also comprehend.

Nobody functions the same way twice. In order to reach a more productive communication space and resolve everything, you're attempting to determine what you both need and how you can help each other to cool down. However, you can't accomplish that if you're still engaged in a heated fight.

Five tried-and-true techniques for interacting peacefully

Can we then put an end to our fighting and start talking? By reducing your physical defense reaction, you need to reactivate that area of your brain. But isn't it true that it's simpler to say than to do?

It takes time and effort to get there. However, as you work on these communication techniques together, you'll start to notice results and get to the point where you can discuss any issues in your relationship with your partner without getting into a fight.

What you must do is as follows:

Part I #1: Determine what you need.

First, be certain that you are entirely aware of the purpose of your argument. Knowing what works best for you can help you return to a baseline where your logical mind is once again operational.

When you feel locked in the "fight or flight" state, there are many strategies to re-calibrate.

When you're unhappy, take a moment to sit down and ask yourself, "What calms me down?"

This could involve playing with your dog, phoning a friend, taking a brief walk, or listening to music. Everyone's version of the proper response is unique, but it's critical that you remember this every time you find yourself in a cycle of conflict.

How to determine what you need

Also, here are five questions to ask yourself to determine what you really need.

It could be helpful to think about your motivations if you're not obtaining the outcomes you "need" in a certain area of your life.

I. Consider this question: Why do I want this result?

"Why" is the most important question we could possibly ponder. The necessity of understanding the motivation behind our actions has been stressed by philosophers and scientists throughout history, from the German philosopher Frederick Neitzsche, who once said, "He who has a why can suffer any how," to Simon Sinek in his book Start With Why. We pursue our goals with passion and tenacity and are much more likely to succeed when these motivations are internal to us and significant to us.

II. What Will I Stand to Gain if I Acquire It?

Because of shifting circumstances and unforeseen events, getting from where we are to where we want to be is not always a straightforward journey. But because of the conflicting desires inherent in our human dilemma, the true battle is frequently inside. The pleasure-seeking self seeks the immediate high, whereas the meaning-making self-works toward future fulfillment. Making a list of all the benefits we receive from reaching our goals might help us stay totally dedicated to our efforts and enjoy the rewards even as we put in the necessary effort.

III. What Would I Lose if I Attained It?

However brilliant and appealing the advantages may seem, there are times when the cost of the effort outweighs that of the gains. This is due to the fact that we also worry about losing unspoken fears. So cultivate a genuine interest by asking yourself, "What do I get by remaining where I am?" and "What do I lose by changing?"

IV. How Would I Feel If I Did Nothing?

It is important to keep in mind that, despite Newton's law of inertia, things cannot remain the same for an extended period of time when the fear of change outweighs the fear of remaining the same. If we do nothing, things frequently get worse because life applies its own imbalanced force to us. Writing out how horrible things could eventually get if you do nothing could be the inspiration you need to continue the cycle of change if you have faith in the conclusion you seek.

V. Consider this: What If I Am Successful?

The ability to imagine is both a gift and a curse. We frequently invent apocalyptic scenarios in our brains to frighten us into inaction or running away because of our intrinsic negative bias. Instead, if we used it to visualize the ideal conclusion for ourselves, we would put ourselves in a state of positive emotional attraction that gives us hope and optimism. Additionally, relating it to the current circumstance gives momentum and prepares the ground for action.

Ambivalence and doubt are common on the path to change. We advance fully towards our objectives when we are sincere in our curiosity about our aspirations, imaginative in our imagination, and motivated in our motivations.

Part II #2: Allow the storm to pass

It can be tempting to attempt to resolve everything immediately when things are tense. However, one of the worst times to do it is, unfortunately, during or right after a disagreement!

It's much more difficult to move toward a true solution when you're in a defensive state, arguing and shouting.

When you are both furious and disturbed, neither of you will speak in a way that will help the situation change since your minds are preoccupied with defending you from a threat rather than learning and comprehending.

Give yourselves some space and time to unwind instead before you sit down to analyze what happened. Before attempting to fix your situation, give yourself some time to calm down and some time to pass. Then, when you're ready to chat, you may continue on to our following advice on how to tell your spouse what you need.

How to allow the storm to pass

The same may be said of relationships. The beginning of the ascension is sometimes the most thrilling stage because you start off on the high of infatuation and are carefree in your short-term objectives.

However, it is how you handle the decline, the bends and twists, and any unexpected drops that threaten to separate you that determines whether or not a relationship will succeed.

My nine-year wedding anniversary was this past week. My spouse and I have experienced numerous low points, yet we continue to move up in our relationship every year.

How does our union function as a rock-solid foundation?

All I know is that if you want a relationship to last, you need to give and receive love in return. You also need to have the appropriate mentality and a realistic outlook on life.

Aim for Imperfections

There is no such thing as the ideal partner; you may have a checklist of qualities to look for in a spouse, some deal-breakers, or guidelines to follow. We all have flaws, nasty sides, or a troubled background that we'd rather burn the pages of our life tale to.

When two people are still in love, they may accept one another's flaws as they are and choose to look past them, even when ugly things happen.

Love isn't aesthetically pleasing all the time, but it is when you develop a stronger bond with your partner over time. You have to fall in love with the same person repeatedly. It must be returned in kind.

Reflect Hidden Advantages

At your utterly pitiful worst, knowing your past, your character traits, and everything that makes you tick provides someone close to you with the ability to bring out the best in you while simultaneously providing the chance to witness you at your utterly pitiful worst.

My postpartum depression and anxiety were really bad after the birth of our first kid. Deeply ingrained trauma was resurfacing, leaving me full of self-doubt and preventing me from completely appreciating motherhood and, ultimately, life. I changed into a new person. It damaged our marriage and was one of the most difficult times for me.

In addition, I despised the damage that pregnancy had done to my body, but it was my husband who told me that he didn't mind and that I should be proud of who I had become.

Even when I wasn't behaving or looking like myself, he stood with me.

Love your partner despite their mental and physical wounds when they don't like what they see in the mirror. When you recognize something in someone, especially if they are unaware of it, you can reflect on it more clearly.

Understand Your Differences and Triggers

I had glaring insecurities as a result of my past and our relationship with my ex, which I projected onto my husband.

Work on yourself from the inside out; while your partner may be able to assist you with your baggage, it is not their responsibility to fix you.

In order to avoid having a negative reaction, don't be scared to express your dislikes and deal with them right away. Sometimes, until you move in together, you won't know.

My husband gets angry anytime I leave the hairdryer plugged in when it isn't in use, and I detest it when he doesn't rinse the dishes after he puts them in the sink.

Out of respect for one another, we make an attempt to change our pet peeves even when they initially appear insignificant. It merely requires us to correct small negative habits; it doesn't force us to change.

Choose Your Battles

Your partner and you will occasionally disagree, and they may even annoy or even irritate you. Rifts are created by little issues, which become worse if left to linger.

Arguments cannot be completely avoided and are occasionally even necessary.

Find out the cause of anything that is causing you to feel bad. Although fighting for a valid purpose might help you connect and grow stronger, fighting for no good reason drives a rift between couples.

If a couple is angry with one another, they are never in the mood for intimacy. I've discovered that there won't be any physical strain if your emotional demands are addressed.

It is accurate to say that "There is no love without forgiveness, and there is no forgiveness without love." Once a disagreement is over, try not to keep track of any wrongdoings and move on. Things will be much easier to forgive than to hold grudges, so work it out so you don't bring it up in the future.

Be there

Once, I was upset about something my husband had said, but I waited until the kids were asleep because I knew it would be best not to argue in front of them.

We need to chat, I said as I headed downstairs to where he was watching TV in the living room. He switched it off silently and turned to face me on the couch.

We don't use our phones while we're out or eating so that we can focus more on one another.

When necessary, take each other seriously and listen to one another with empathy. Avoid listening in a disinterested or passive manner.

Communication That Works

I used to scream and shout when I was angry before we had fully developed together, which did nothing but exacerbate the problem.

No matter how unpleasant the subject is, my husband and I now initiate dialogue, take turns giving our thoughts, and discuss things. It shows I'm confident enough to open up about anything without worrying about being judged. I might say, for example:

"I became angry because..."

"It made me feel bad when you..."

"I apologize that,"

Most people have trouble reading signs. Would you rather have someone state their issue clearly to you rather than leave you in the dark and act passive-aggressively?

Use your words carefully and with purpose. Be sincere and forthright. Display sensitivity I genuinely apologize.

Being seen and heard allows one to feel loved and supported. Always pay attention to what is being said, but accepting others for who they truly are is much more crucial. Proper communication is the first step in demonstrating your care, and this is done in addition to using your actions, which always convey more meaning than words.

Avoid family conflicts

If you're thinking about getting married, even if you're really in love with your significant other, will your relationship withstand the fury of your family or a future in-law who doesn't approve?

That's great if you get along during holiday gatherings and exchange niceties, but can you see yourself spending the rest of your life with each other? Family drama frequently causes partnerships to fall apart.

In order to establish your limits and where to draw any lines early on, it can be helpful to talk about your future together and consider potential scenarios when you are ready. You can compromise occasionally, but not always.

Maintain Distance

To paraphrase one of my favorite Boyz II Men songs,

"Even deeply in love, individuals need time apart from one another."

Setting aside time for quality time and participating in activities as a pair is wonderful. Even so, if you plan to spend the rest of your days together, it is advisable to maintain a healthy balance between independence and dependence by having a distinct existence, whether it be a social circle or some unrelated interests.

In order to give each other freedom and space, you also need trust, which is the cornerstone of any lasting relationship and must be gained.

Continue dating.

You don't have to feel like you've aged or get tired of the same old, same old if you've been together for a while.

I stayed at a hot spring resort over the new year's break and leased out a room equipped for playing table tennis. I was watching my husband teach me how to smash a ping pong ball when I started to remember our very first date, which was more than ten years ago.

In order to get behind me and close enough for the aroma of his cologne to make me feel butterflies, he had taken me to the driving range and taught me how to play golf properly.

We had this conversation that night when we were lying next to each other on the futon, and it speaks volumes about how connected we are. First, I said,

Table tennis was enjoyable today.

Was it not? I'm happy that we were able to rent the space.

"Did you have any thoughts when you were playing?"

"Golf."

Together, go on a trip down memory lane. Take your date out on a vintage-style date. It will rekindle old emotions with the same lovely butterflies, and it will bring back pleasant memories.

Pay attention to the details

Although my hubby does not have a romantic side, I can still see it.

When I'm acting sleepy, he kisses my forehead. When I'm ill, he fills the fridge with electrolyte drinks and fresh fruit. And in the cold, he's obsessed with keeping me warm.

He keeps winning me over with these little things he does.

Your spouse will show you love in special ways. Remember them and show appreciation.

Never assume anything about one another.

There are times in a long-term relationship when you become overly cozy and complacent. If you become fixated on everything you do for the other person, it might sometimes even be with resentment.

The best way to express thankfulness is to acknowledge that you don't get to do something because you have to; rather, you get to do it because you get to.

You will be on your way to greater heights in your relationship as long as your goals for the future are in sync and you both put in the effort.

Real love is both enchanted and useful. If you can see it for all that it is, you most certainly have something exceptional, and it couldn't get any better with anybody else, barring irreconcilable disagreements. Treasuring it all.

We may not always agree, but when we work together, we do.

When all is said and done

I'll always remember how I first met my husband and the excitement of the journey, but you shouldn't base the durability of your relationship just on your sentiments. The honeymoon period ends quickly.

Relationships provide a window into who we are, and that is how you and your partner evolve. Sticking together through thick and thin is what commitment means.

One thing I always consider when it comes to our marriage is how we've survived all the difficult times. When it counts most, it's how your partner is there for you when you least expect it.

Part III #3: Be clear about what you require.

It's simple to believe that your lover knows what you're thinking when you've been dating them for a while. However, what you need may not necessarily be what your partner needs, and sadly, none of us can read minds (at least, I haven't come across any couples who do!).

Inform your partner once you are aware of what brings you back to your center of gravity.

Your partner will better understand you and your requirements if you are specific in stating "when I'm sad, I need X." Conversely, work on your active listening techniques and pay attention to what your partner needs from your disagreements.

Here's an illustration: "I need to go outside for a brief walk when I'm truly unhappy. I require my own room. Or, alternatively, "I truly need you to be with me, give me a hug, and tell me that everything's okay when I'm upset." This kind of transparency with your partner is crucial, and you should also be receptive to learning about their requirements.

By sharing with one another, you can get to the point where you can all work together to overcome bad communication.

How to be clear about what you require.

Here is how to decide what you want in a relationship in 10 simple stages

Knowing what you desire from a spouse demands self-awareness and a determination of your basic principles as well as what you cannot compromise on. Although it might seem easy, doing this can be really difficult.

To make the process simpler, there are ten steps you may take to determine what you want in a relationship.

Identify and list your main principles.

You'll have to look within and honestly assess why you want to do this. You should make a list of the things you have desired from relationships throughout your life, say dating gurus.

Look for recurring patterns since they can point to the fundamental principles or characteristics that symbolize what you value in a partner.

Analyze previous connections

You can determine what you enjoy and don't like in a relationship by looking back on previous relationships. If anything goes wrong in a previous relationship, you can learn what to avoid in future ones.

However, examining the aspects of a past relationship you miss can help you identify the qualities you are seeking in a partner.

Use the values you have from other categories to decide what to look for.

Finding out what you want in a relationship can be aided by knowing what you value in your profession or financial life.

For instance, if you value routine in your everyday life and a 9 to 5 work schedule, you should look for a partner who can support this.

Investigate and consider what you desire in a relationship.

Do not rush into marriage and the search for the ideal companion. It could take a few failed relationships or dates for you to figure out what you do and do not want in a partner.

Be alert to warning signs

We have all felt that queasy sensation in our gut when dating someone who is simply not right for us.

Whether it's anything they say or the way they make us feel, those feelings can indicate warning signs, which can be very helpful in letting us know what we don't want in a partner.

Focus on relationships you value.

You probably have at least one couple in mind whom you admire for their happy marriage or the way they view one another.

For a moment, think about what it is about this relationship that appeals to you. Is it the way they help one another out when things get tough? How do they converse with one another?

You can use these hints to guide your decision on what kind of relationship you want.

Put your own needs first.

You will ultimately settle for less than what you deserve if you don't value yourself and don't think you deserve to get what you want in a relationship.

It is easy to become preoccupied with making sure you fulfill your partner's needs and desires, but if you don't value yourself, your own objectives may suffer.

You will be able to recognize what you want and won't be afraid to ask for it from your spouse if you value yourself and see yourself as a "reward" for the correct relationship.

Try out this self-awareness activity.

This self-awareness practice is advised by experts as it might help you figure out what you desire in a partner. Think about the qualities you want in a spouse. Put your eyes closed and give it your all.

When you're finished, look around you and write down all the characteristics you see. Take some time to consider each quality and decide whether it is something you can live without or something you appreciate.

Mark a quality with an "E" to indicate that it is absolutely necessary if it is non-negotiable. Other qualities on the list may be traits you appreciate but don't need in a relationship, whereas essential attributes are what you desire in a partnership.

Do not be frightened to be by yourself occasionally.

Take a break from dating and spend some time on your own if you have already tried other methods to figure out what you want in a relationship but are still unclear about the answer.

This provides you plenty of time to ponder who you are and what you want from a partner. It's crucial to explore and do what you want when you're single in order to figure out what you enjoy and don't like.

This reveals important details about your relationship needs.

Never enter into a relationship unless you are sure of what you want.

Experts advise against entering into a relationship without knowing what you want. Make a list of the qualities you look for in a mate and keep it handy for starting new relationships.

If not, you could strive to modify your partner over the course of the relationship in order to make them more accommodating. Successful results from this are rare.

Part IV #4: Convey a strategy.

It's crucial to consider what your partner wants at that specific time in the argument when you're both agitated and need to settle down.

Decide on a single thing you're both willing to do by working with your partner.

You'll be better able to assist each other in settling the following disagreement more quickly if you can decide on one thing to attempt.

Every pair has a unique way of communicating. I really need to know that you're paying attention and that you care about this, for instance, if you spoke to your partner. I become anxious when you turn away from me.

The response from your spouse can be, "I agreed to let you know that I need space and that I'm not leaving the argument." Even if I want to solve this, my mind isn't in the correct frame of mind at the moment. Before I can fully consider this, I need to go for a stroll.

Knowing these predetermined plans in advance will assist in defusing the situation and bring both of you back to a state of calm where a resolution can be achieved.

How to Convey a Strategy

In a healthy relationship, honesty, trust, respect, and open communication are essential components in conveying a strategy to your partner. It also requires effort and compromise from both sides. No power disparity exists. Partners respect one another's freedom, are free to act independently without fear of repercussions or criticism, and work together to make decisions.

Part V #5: Appreciate your partner's work.

Great partnerships need mutual work, so it's critical to acknowledge your partner for their contributions as well.

Next time you argue, take a moment to appreciate the effort your partner is making.

Be sure to point out any adjustments they are making that are enhancing your mutual communication. For instance, "I really appreciate you trying that." Thank you. " When we're both upset, I know it's difficult for you to give me space, but doing so allowed me to calm down and talk about this.

When your partner tries something new, especially if it can be challenging for them, saying how much you appreciate them can go a long way toward fostering good communication and preventing future arguments.

It is never easy to resist the need to defend yourself when you are already angry or offended.

However, by practicing these communication skills, you may hopefully transition from an environment of escalating conflict and unintentionally cruel language to one of calmer discourse where you can use the logical side of your brain to make progress in the future on some of those concerns.

How to appreciate your partner's work

Here are ten ways to appreciate your partner

Gratitude is a habit that should be practiced every day in order to maintain a happy marriage. In this book, I'm going to share 10 possible suggestions for thanking your spouse or wife, but there are many other ways as well.

Say it out loud and more often!

The easiest and most straightforward way to express your thanks to your spouse is to say "thank you" more frequently. It's simple to forget to express gratitude to your spouse for little, seemingly unimportant chores. But you'll discover that, especially if your partner has been feeling overwhelmed, your thankfulness can change the way he or she perceives these responsibilities. It doesn't take much work, yet just two straightforward words have a big impact.

Send an intemperate card, note, or letter.

Write a thank-you note and put it wherever your spouse can quickly locate it, like their lunchbox, the dashboard of their car, the bathroom mirror, or a similar location. It's incredible how a simple note can make someone's day. Even writing a message on a sticky note can help them feel more accomplished in their everyday tasks.

Permit Your Wife a Break.

If your spouse is overworked or raising young children, a few hours of solitude may very well be at the top of their list of desires. Or perhaps they simply need a break from their routine duties. Give them the chance to take that much-needed break, whether it's a few hours to curl up with a book or your taking over their chores for the day. (If you are a parent, get child care or look after the kids yourself.)

Make a unique dinner.

Has your partner ever had a dish they just adored making or a recipe they have been longing to try? Do you occasionally prepare a meal that both of you like and that brings back fond memories? Set aside some time to make a homemade meal exclusively for him or her. Dinner is served at home while you listen to music and light some candles.

Honor him or her in front of your children, then get them involved.

Your children will pick up on your thankfulness for your spouse if you express it to (and in front of) them! Spend some time intentionally telling your children all the wonderful things your spouse does for the family, and encourage them to express their gratitude to their other parent as well. You may even take it a step further and advise that the kids do handmade artwork as a way to express their gratitude to their parents or that they even assist with household duties in order to lighten the strain on your spouse. Your entire immediate family will benefit if you teach your kids to be grateful.

To the world, describe what your wife does for you.

Go a little outside the confines of your home and express your gratitude for your spouse as frequently as you can to others. Tell people about it in your large family, your friends, or at church. Utilize your social media accounts to express your gratitude for all that your spouse does for you and your family.

Be honest and grateful.

It's not quite enough to say "thank you," give gifts, and tell others about your spouse; you also need to act in a thankful manner toward them. Make an effort to pay attention to what they do and acknowledge the effort they put forth for you, whether they are managing the household, a business, or both. Don't regard him or her as a given. Make sure you are careful and cautious to avoid undermining or damaging their work in any manner.

Go on a romantic date with your spouse.

A romantic date is a wonderful way to appreciate your spouse for everything they do for you. Pick their favorite eatery, a movie they've wanted to watch, get a coffee, go for a walk in the woods, or visit their preferred bookshop or library. Make your spouse the focus of that time.

Give a gift just for fun.

Sometimes a token of appreciation is appropriate. Then purchase something your spouse would appreciate but might not be able to afford, and attach a little message of appreciation before giving it to them. It's possible that your husband has been coveting a watch or a pair of cufflinks, or that your wife has her eye on a book or a movie that she hasn't purchased for herself. This can be the ideal time to treat him or her to something special.

Aim to provide more than you receive.

In order to have a happy marriage, you must be a servant. Avoiding acting solely as a "taker" is another approach to expressing your gratitude. Give, give, give—your partner is giving to you, so be sure to not just return the favor but go above and above. And be sure to give selflessly, without anticipating anything in return.